Fairways & Femininity

modern woman's guide to golf

Written by Stacey Soans

Copyright 2025 Stacey Soans All Rights Reserved

This book is subject to the condition that no part of this book is to
be reproduced, transmitted in any form or means, electronic or mechanical, stored in a retrieval system, photocopied, recorded, scanned, or otherwise. Any of these actions require the proper written permission of the author.

Published by **Book Writing Craft**, 4900 California Avenue, Tower B, 2nd Floor, Bakersfield, CA 93309 **877-286-0704**

Dedication

To my incredible parents, Mr. and Mrs. Soans,

Your journey from India to Canada was one of courage, sacrifice, and unwavering determination. You built a life from the ground up, creating opportunities not just for yourselves but for me—to dream, to grow, and to become the person I am today. This book is a testament to the values you instilled in me—the importance of hard work, perseverance, and believing in one's dreams. Every page of this book is a testament to the foundation you built and the love and support that have guided me along the way.

To my golf instructors,

Thank you for your patience, guidance, and the countless lessons—both on and off the course. Your dedication to the game and your belief in my progress have shaped not just my swing, but my appreciation for the sport itself. Every round, every challenge, and every small victory is a reflection of the time and effort you've invested in me.

With all my love and gratitude,

Stacey

Table of Contents

Chapter 1: The Rise of Women's Golf in the Modern Era 1

Chapter 2: Fashion Meets Function - The Evolution of Women's Golf Apparel and Culture 12

Chapter 3: The Best Golf Courses for Women Worldwide 20

Chapter 4: Empowering Women & Building Community 31

Chapter 5: The Ultimate Woman's Golf Travel Guide 43

Chapter 6: The Bond Between Women and Golf: Community and Connection 60

Chapter 7: Balancing Life and the Fairway: The Multidimensional Woman Golfer 66

About the Author 73

Chapter 1:
The Rise of Women's Golf in the Modern Era

Women's golf has entered a new and exciting chapter, marked by a surge in global popularity, record-breaking performances, and groundbreaking opportunities for female athletes. Once overshadowed by the men's game, women's golf now commands increasing attention from fans, sponsors, and media outlets alike. The modern era of women's golf is defined by innovation, talent, and unprecedented financial investment, creating an environment where female golfers can thrive like never before.

This chapter explores the rise of women's golf in the 21st century, focusing on its transformation into a premier global sport. From the emergence of new stars to advances in technology and the booming business of women's golf, we will examine the key factors that have propelled the game forward.

How Golf Became Popular With Women

The origins of golf are shrouded in the mists of Scottish history, with the game evolving from a rudimentary pastime played with sticks and stones into the structured sport we recognize today. While the early history of golf is often dominated by male figures, women were not absent from the game. In fact, they were present almost from the beginning, though their participation was often informal and undocumented.

The first recorded mention of women playing golf dates back to the 16th century. In Scotland, golf was not just a sport but a social activity, and women of the upper classes were known to participate alongside men. The game was played on public lands, often referred to as "links," which were stretches of sandy, undulating terrain near the coast. These links were communal spaces where people of all ages and genders could gather, and it was here that women first began to swing clubs.

One of the earliest references to a woman golfer comes from the town of St. Andrews, often called the "home of golf." In 1552, the Archbishop of St. Andrews issued a decree allowing the townspeople to play golf on the links, and there is evidence to suggest that women were among those who took advantage of this privilege. While their names have been lost to history, their presence on the links is a testament to the inclusive nature of early golf.

Beyond Scotland, women were also playing golf in other parts of Europe. In the Netherlands, a game similar to golf called "kolf" was popular among both men and women as early as the 13th century. Dutch paintings from the 17th century depict women playing kolf in leisurely settings, suggesting that the game was seen as a socially acceptable activity for women. While kolf and golf are distinct games, the Dutch influence on Scottish golf is well-documented, and it is likely that the participation of women in kolf helped pave the way for their involvement in golf.

19th-Century Pioneers and the First Women's Golf Clubs

The 19th century marked a turning point for women in golf. As the sport became more organized and formalized, women began to carve out a space for themselves within it. This period saw the emergence of the first women's golf clubs, as well as the rise of female pioneers who pushed the boundaries of what was considered acceptable for women in sport.

One of the earliest women's golf clubs was the St. Andrews Ladies' Putting Club, founded in 1867. The club was established in response to the growing number of women who wanted to play golf but were excluded from the existing clubs. At the time, it was considered unseemly for women to take full swings, so the St. Andrews Ladies' Putting Club focused exclusively on putting. This allowed women to participate in the sport while adhering to the strict social norms of the time. The club was an instant success, attracting members from across Scotland and beyond.

The establishment of the St. Andrews Ladies' Putting Club was a significant milestone, but it was only the beginning. In 1893, the Ladies' Golf Union (LGU) was founded in the United Kingdom, becoming the first governing body for women's golf. The LGU organized the first British Ladies' Amateur Championship in 1893, which was won by Lady Margaret Scott. This event marked the beginning of competitive women's golf and helped to raise the profile of the sport.

Across the Atlantic, women in the United States were also making strides in golf. The first women's golf club in the U.S., the Morristown Golf Club in New Jersey, was founded in 1894. Like its Scottish counterpart, the Morristown Golf Club initially focused on putting, but it soon expanded to include full rounds of golf. The club's founder, Mary Browne, was a passionate advocate for women's golf and worked tirelessly to promote the sport.

The late 19th century also saw the emergence of female golfing stars who challenged societal norms and inspired future generations. One such figure was Issette Pearson, a prominent British golfer who won the British Ladies' Amateur Championship in 1896. Pearson was known for her powerful swing and competitive spirit, qualities that were often discouraged in women at the time. Her success helped to dispel the notion that golf was a game best suited to men.

Pioneers in Petticoats: The Women Who Redefined the Game

Beyond their contributions on the course, women played a significant role in shaping the culture of golf. As the sport grew in popularity, women became involved in organizing tournaments, managing clubs, and promoting the game to a wider audience. Their efforts helped to establish golf as a social activity that could be enjoyed by people of all ages and backgrounds.

One notable example of this is the role of women in the development of golf etiquette. The emphasis on sportsmanship, respect, and integrity that characterizes modern golf can be traced back to the early days of the sport, when women played a key role in establishing these values. By promoting a culture of fairness and respect, women helped to ensure that golf remained a game that could be enjoyed by all.

The early history of women's involvement in the sport of golf shows two qualities within the early female golfers, perseverance and passion. From the windswept links of Scotland to the first women's golf clubs, female golfers have fought to claim their place in a sport that was not always welcoming. Their journey has been marked by challenges and triumphs, but through it all, they have remained steadfast in their love for the game.

As we look back on the early history of women's golf, it is impossible not to be inspired by the courage and determination of those who came before. They were pioneers in every sense of the word, breaking down barriers and paving the way for future generations of female golfers. Their legacy is one of resilience and hope, a reminder that the love of the game knows no bounds.

A Shift in the Spotlight: The New Superstars of Women's Golf

In recent years, the competitive landscape of women's golf has evolved dramatically. The sport is no longer dominated by a handful of elite players; instead, it boasts an impressive depth of talent from around the world. Unlike past decades, where one or two players commanded most of the attention, today's women's golf features multiple rising stars who are changing the way the game is played.

Take, for example, Nelly Korda, the American golfer who has become a household name with her effortless swing and commanding performances on the LPGA Tour. With multiple tournament wins, including major championships, she has cemented her place among the world's best. Similarly, South Korea's Jin Young Ko has consistently showcased her dominance, with multiple victories and a reputation for impeccable precision.

Beyond these established stars, the game is filled with young, up-and-coming players who are ready to challenge for the top spot. Thailand's Atthaya Thitikul, who rose to the No. 1 ranking at just 19 years old, is part of a new wave of fearless golfers redefining what is possible. Lydia Ko, once a teenage sensation, continues to be a force on the course, proving that longevity in the sport is achievable with skill, dedication, and adaptability.

The diversity in today's women's golf scene is another defining feature of its success. The LPGA Tour and other women's golf circuits now showcase players from all over the world, from Europe to Asia, North America to Australia. This has made women's golf truly international, with different styles of play, cultural influences, and competitive approaches enriching the game.

With the rise of social media, these athletes are more connected to their fans than ever before. They regularly share glimpses of their training routines, personal lives, and tournament experiences, making them more relatable and accessible. As a result, women's golf is no longer just about what happens on the course; it's about building global icons who inspire the next generation.

The Business of Women's Golf: A Game-Changer

The financial landscape of women's golf has changed dramatically over the past two decades. While female golfers once struggled for recognition and financial backing, the tide has shifted, and today's players benefit from major sponsorship deals, increased prize purses, and growing media coverage.

The LPGA Tour has seen a dramatic increase in total prize money, with the 2023 season boasting over $100 million in purses—a record-breaking number. The U.S. Women's Open at Pebble Beach set a new standard with a $10 million prize fund, signaling a turning point for women's professional golf. This level of financial support ensures that today's female golfers can make a lucrative career from the sport, allowing them to focus entirely on training and competing at the highest level.

Beyond tournament winnings, sponsorships play a huge role in shaping the modern era of women's golf. Leading golf equipment companies such as Titleist, Callaway, and Ping are investing in female players like never before, creating signature clubs and gear designed specifically for women. Meanwhile, luxury brands, fitness companies, and lifestyle influencers have recognized the marketing power of female golfers, further expanding their endorsement opportunities.

The success of the LPGA Tour has also inspired other women's golf circuits worldwide. The Ladies European Tour (LET), the Japan LPGA Tour, and the Korea LPGA Tour have all experienced growth in sponsorship and prize money, providing more playing opportunities for female golfers around the world.

This influx of investment is not only benefiting elite players but also helping to grow the game at the grassroots level. More funding is being directed toward junior golf programs, ensuring that young girls have access to coaching, equipment, and tournament experience from an early age. As more girls take up golf, the future of the sport looks even brighter.

Training and Technology: The Evolution of the Modern Golfer

Women's golf has become more competitive than ever, thanks in part to advancements in technology and training methodologies. Today's female golfers train like elite athletes, focusing on physical fitness, mental conditioning, and precision in ways that were once reserved for male professionals.

Strength and conditioning programs have become a staple for modern players, helping them increase swing speed, power, and endurance. Unlike the past, when golf was seen as a purely skill-based sport, today's players incorporate weightlifting, flexibility training, and cardiovascular workouts into their routines to optimize their performance.

Swing analysis and biomechanical studies have also transformed the way golfers train. High-speed cameras, launch monitors, and artificial intelligence-powered coaching tools allow players to fine-tune their swings with incredible accuracy. Golf simulators provide virtual practice sessions on world-famous courses, giving players the ability to prepare for tournaments in ways that were previously impossible.

The evolution of golf equipment has played a crucial role in improving the women's game as well. Custom-fitted clubs designed for female golfers have become the norm, allowing players to maximize their strengths on the course. Golf ball technology has also advanced, helping players achieve greater distance and control.

The modern female golfer is not just a talented ball-striker; she is an athlete in every sense of the word. The combination of skill, fitness, strategy, and technology has elevated the women's game to a level never seen before.

Global Expansion: The Reach of Women's Golf Beyond the U.S.

One of the most remarkable aspects of the modern era is the truly global nature of women's golf. Once seen as a sport dominated by a few countries, golf now thrives on nearly every continent.

Asia, in particular, has become a powerhouse in the women's game. South Korea continues to produce world-class players, thanks to its strong golf culture and emphasis on discipline and technique. Thailand has also emerged as a dominant force, with players like Ariya Jutanugarn and Patty Tavatanakit winning on the LPGA Tour.

Japan's golf scene has flourished in recent years, with tournaments drawing massive crowds and the country's top female players becoming national icons. Meanwhile, China and

India are beginning to develop strong junior programs, signaling that the next generation of talent may come from unexpected places.

Europe has long been a key player in women's golf, and its influence continues to grow. The Ladies European Tour has expanded its reach, hosting tournaments in the Middle East and Africa, while the Solheim Cup, the women's equivalent of the Ryder Cup, remains one of the most exciting team competitions in the sport.

With golf's inclusion in the Olympics, the global appeal of the sport has only strengthened. More countries are investing in women's golf programs, ensuring that the sport's growth will continue for years to come.

Looking Ahead: The Future of Women's Golf

With so much momentum behind women's golf, the future looks incredibly bright. Increased media coverage ensures that more people than ever are watching tournaments, while digital platforms allow fans to engage with the game in new ways.

Streaming services have made it easier to watch women's golf worldwide, giving fans unprecedented access to tournaments. Meanwhile, social media has enabled female golfers to build personal brands, connect with sponsors, and interact directly with their followers.

As technology continues to evolve, training methods will become even more advanced, pushing the limits of what is possible on the course. Players will continue to hit the ball farther, play more aggressively, and bring excitement to every tournament.

Perhaps most importantly, the perception of women's golf is changing. No longer seen as an afterthought to the men's game, women's golf is establishing itself as a premier sporting spectacle in its own right. With continued investment, innovation, and star power, it's only a matter of time before women's golf reaches heights never before imagined.

Chapter 2:
Fashion Meets Function - The Evolution of Women's Golf Apparel and Culture

Golf has long been associated with tradition, but in recent years, the sport has undergone a dramatic transformation, especially for women. No longer confined to rigid dress codes and outdated styles, women's golf has embraced a new era of fashion, elegance, and fun. This chapter explores the rise of modern golf apparel brands that blend fashion with functionality and examines how the culture of women's golf has shifted from a rigid, male-dominated space to one that celebrates individuality, inclusivity, and enjoyment.

The Best Modern Golf Apparel Brands That Mix Fashion with Functionality

Golf fashion has evolved from the days of boxy polos and ill-fitting skirts to a vibrant industry that prioritizes both style and performance. Today, women's golf apparel is designed to empower players, offering comfort, mobility, and a touch of elegance. Here are some of the top brands leading the charge in modern golf fashion:

1. Nike Golf

Nike has long been a leader in athletic wear, and its golf line is no exception. The brand's women's golf collection combines cutting-edge technology with sleek, modern designs. From moisture-wicking polo shirts to tailored skirts and pants, Nike Golf offers pieces that are both functional and fashionable. The brand's use of Dri-FIT technology ensures that players stay cool and dry on the course, while its bold color palettes and minimalist designs appeal to a wide range of tastes.

Nike has also embraced the athleisure trend, creating pieces that transition seamlessly from the course to casual outings. Their sleeveless tops, leggings, and lightweight jackets are perfect for women who want to look stylish both on and off the green.

2. Adidas Golf

Adidas Golf is another major player in the women's golf apparel market. Known for its innovative fabrics and sporty aesthetic, Adidas offers a range of clothing that combines performance with style. The brand's Climacool technology ensures breathability, while its tailored fits provide a polished look.

Adidas has also made strides in inclusivity, offering extended sizes and designs that cater to women of all body types. Their collaboration with influencers and professional golfers has helped to modernize their image, making them a favorite among younger players.

3. Lululemon

While Lululemon is best known for its yoga and activewear, the brand has made significant inroads into the golf market. Their women's golf collection features stretchy, moisture-wicking fabrics that allow for maximum mobility and comfort. Lululemon's sleek, minimalist designs are perfect for women who want to look chic on the course without sacrificing performance.

The brand's focus on versatility is another major draw. Many of their golf pieces can be worn for other activities, making them a practical choice for women with active lifestyles.

4. G/FORE

G/FORE has quickly become a favorite among fashion-forward golfers. Known for its bold patterns, vibrant colors, and playful designs, G/FORE offers a refreshing departure from traditional golf apparel. The brand's gloves, in particular, have gained a cult following for their unique prints and high-quality materials.

G/FORE's clothing line is equally impressive, featuring tailored polos, skirts, and pants that combine style with functionality. The brand's commitment to individuality and self-expression has made it a hit among younger players and influencers.

5. Galvin Green

For women who prioritize performance, Galvin Green is a top choice. The Swedish brand is known for its high-tech fabrics and weather-resistant designs, making it a favorite among serious golfers. While their aesthetic is more understated than some other brands, Galvin Green's attention to detail and commitment to quality make them a standout in the industry.

Galvin Green has also embraced the trend toward more fitted, feminine silhouettes, offering pieces that flatter the female form without compromising on performance.

6. RLX Ralph Lauren

RLX Ralph Lauren combines classic elegance with modern functionality. The brand's women's golf line features timeless designs, such as pinstripe skirts and tailored blazers, that exude sophistication. RLX also incorporates performance fabrics into its designs, ensuring that players stay comfortable and dry on the course.

The brand's commitment to timeless style makes it a favorite among women who want to look polished and professional while playing.

The Shift from Traditional, Rigid Golf Culture to a More Elegant and Fun Experience for Women

For much of its history, golf was seen as a male-dominated sport with strict rules and traditions. Women were often relegated to the sidelines, both on the course and in the clubhouse. Dress codes were rigid, and the culture of the sport was anything but inclusive. However, in recent years, there has been a significant shift toward making golf more accessible, enjoyable, and welcoming for women.

1. Breaking Down Dress Codes

One of the most visible changes in women's golf has been the relaxation of dress codes. While many clubs still have rules in place, there has been a growing movement toward more flexible and inclusive policies. Women are no longer required to wear skirts or adhere to outdated standards of "appropriate" attire. Instead, they are free to choose clothing that makes them feel comfortable and confident.

This shift has been driven in part by the rise of modern golf apparel brands, which have shown that performance and style can coexist. Women are now able to express their individuality through their clothing, whether that means wearing bold patterns, vibrant colors, or sleek, minimalist designs.

2. The Rise of Women's Leagues and Social Events

Another major change in women's golf has been the rise of leagues and social events designed specifically for women. These organizations provide a supportive and inclusive environment where women can learn, play, and connect with others who share their passion for the sport.

Events like the LPGA's Women's Golf Day and the PGA's Girls Golf initiative have played a key role in encouraging women to take up the sport. These programs offer clinics, networking opportunities, and social gatherings that make golf more approachable and enjoyable.

Women's leagues have also become increasingly popular, providing a space for players of all skill levels to compete and socialize. These leagues often include fun, non-competitive elements, such as themed tournaments and post-round gatherings, that emphasize the social aspect of the game.

3. The Influence of Social Media and Influencers

Social media has played a pivotal role in transforming the culture of women's golf. Platforms like Instagram, TikTok, and YouTube have given female golfers a voice and a platform to share their experiences, connect with fans, and inspire others.

Influencers like Paige Spiranac and Blair O'Neal have used their platforms to break down stereotypes and show that golf can be fun, fashionable, and inclusive. Their influence has helped attract a younger, more diverse audience to the sport, challenging the notion that golf is only for older men.

Social media has also created a sense of community among female golfers. Women are now able to share tips, celebrate milestones, and encourage one another to keep playing, creating a supportive and inclusive environment both online and offline.

4. The Emphasis on Wellness and Relaxation

As golf has become more inclusive, there has been a growing emphasis on wellness and relaxation. Many clubs and resorts now offer amenities specifically designed for women, such as spas, fitness centers, and wellness programs. These additions have transformed golf into a holistic experience that goes beyond the game itself.

For many women, golf is now as much about self-care as it is about competition. The opportunity to unwind at a spa or enjoy a leisurely meal with friends after a round of golf has made the sport more appealing to a wider audience.

5. The Role of Fashion in Redefining Golf Culture

Fashion has played a key role in redefining the culture of women's golf. By offering stylish, functional clothing that allows women to express their individuality, modern golf apparel brands have helped to break down the barriers that once made the sport feel exclusive and intimidating.

The rise of athleisure has also contributed to this shift, blurring the lines between sportswear and everyday fashion. Women are now able to wear golf clothing that feels both practical and fashionable, making the sport more accessible and appealing.

Conclusion: A New Era for Women's Golf

The evolution of women's golf apparel and culture reflects a broader shift toward inclusivity, individuality, and enjoyment. Modern brands have redefined what it means to dress for the course, offering stylish, functional clothing that empowers women to look and feel their best. At the same time, the culture of women's golf has become more welcoming and diverse, breaking down the barriers that once made the sport feel exclusive.

As we look to the future, it's clear that women's golf will continue to evolve, embracing new trends, technologies, and ideas. Whether through fashion, social events, or wellness programs, the sport is becoming a space where women can thrive, connect, and express themselves.

Chapter 3:
The Best Golf Courses for Women Worldwide

North America: Where Tradition Meets Modernity

North America boasts some of the most iconic and female-friendly golf courses in the world. These courses are not only visually stunning but also offer a welcoming environment for women of all skill levels.

Pinehurst Resort – Pinehurst, North Carolina, USA

Pinehurst Resort is a legendary destination for golfers, and its commitment to inclusivity makes it a standout choice for women. The resort features nine courses, with the famed Pinehurst No. 2 being a must-play. Designed by Donald Ross, this course is known for its challenging yet fair layout, making it enjoyable for players of all abilities. Pinehurst also offers women's clinics, leagues, and events, fostering a sense of community among female golfers. The resort's luxurious accommodations and Southern hospitality add to the overall experience, making it a top choice for women seeking both challenge and relaxation.

The Pinehurst No. 4 course, redesigned by Gil Hanse, is another gem, offering a more modern layout with dramatic elevation changes and stunning water features. The resort's commitment to women's golf is evident in its Women's Golf Week, an annual event that includes clinics, social events, and networking opportunities. Pinehurst's rich history, combined with its modern amenities, makes it a must-visit destination for female golfers.

The resort's Cradle Course, a short, fun layout designed by Gil Hanse, is perfect for a relaxed round or a quick game after a day on the main courses. Pinehurst's Thistle Dhu Putting Course is another highlight, offering a playful and social experience for golfers of all skill levels. The resort's Spa at Pinehurst provides a range of wellness treatments, ensuring that female golfers can relax and rejuvenate after a day on the course.

Banff Springs Golf Course – Banff, Alberta, Canada

Nestled in the heart of the Canadian Rockies, Banff Springs Golf Course is a visual masterpiece. Designed by Stanley Thompson, this course offers breathtaking views of snow-capped mountains, dense forests, and the winding Bow River. The course is known for its welcoming atmosphere and thoughtful amenities, including women's tees that provide a fair yet challenging experience. Banff Springs also offers a range of wellness facilities, including a spa and fitness center, making it an ideal destination for women looking to combine golf with relaxation.

The Stanley Thompson 18 is the crown jewel of the resort, featuring iconic holes like the Devil's Cauldron, a par-3 surrounded by towering cliffs and a glacial lake. The course's design ensures that players of all skill levels can enjoy the game, while the resort's luxurious accommodations and fine dining options provide a perfect retreat after a day on the course. Banff Springs' commitment to creating a welcoming environment for women is evident in its tailored programs and events, making it a top choice for female golfers.

The Tunnel Mountain 9 course offers a shorter, more relaxed round, perfect for beginners or those looking for a quick game. The resort's Willow Stream Spa provides a range of wellness treatments, including massages, facials, and hydrotherapy, ensuring that female golfers can unwind and recharge. Banff Springs' combination of natural beauty, luxury, and inclusivity makes it a top destination for female golfers.

Europe: A Blend of History and Elegance

Europe is home to some of the world's most historic and picturesque golf courses. These destinations offer a unique blend of tradition, elegance, and female-friendly amenities.

Evian Resort Golf Club – Évian-les-Bains, France

Located on the shores of Lake Geneva, the Evian Resort Golf Club is a haven for female golfers. This course is the proud host of the Evian Championship, one of the five major tournaments in women's golf. The course itself is a masterpiece, with rolling hills, water features, and stunning views of the lake. Evian Resort also offers a range of amenities tailored to women, including a luxurious spa, fine dining, and wellness programs. The resort's commitment to women's golf is evident in its support of female players and its efforts to create an inclusive environment.

The Evian Championship has played a significant role in elevating the profile of women's golf, attracting top players from around the world. The course's design, by architect Steve

Smyers, ensures a challenging yet enjoyable experience for players of all skill levels. The resort's Evian Spa, with its thermal baths and wellness treatments, provides the perfect way to unwind after a day on the course. Evian Resort's combination of luxury, history, and inclusivity makes it a top destination for female golfers.

The Evian Academy offers tailored instruction programs for women, helping them improve their skills in a supportive environment. The resort's Les Jardins de la Reine restaurant offers gourmet dining with stunning views of the lake, making it the perfect place to relax after a day on the course. Evian Resort's combination of luxury, history, and inclusivity makes it a top destination for female golfers.

St. Andrews – The Castle Course – St. Andrews, Scotland

No list of golf courses would be complete without a mention of St. Andrews, the birthplace of golf. While the Old Course is iconic, the Castle Course offers a more modern and female-friendly experience. Designed by David McLay Kidd, this course features dramatic cliffside views, challenging greens, and a layout that caters to players of all skill levels. St. Andrews is also known for its welcoming atmosphere, with a range of programs and events designed to encourage women to take up the sport. The town itself is steeped in golf history, making it a must-visit destination for any female golfer.

The Castle Course is known for its stunning views of the North Sea and the town of St. Andrews. The course's design incorporates natural features like dunes and cliffs, creating a challenging yet rewarding experience. St. Andrews' commitment to inclusivity is evident in its Women's Golf Week, which includes clinics, social events, and networking opportunities. The town's rich history, combined with its modern amenities, makes it a top choice for female golfers.

The St. Andrews Links Academy offers tailored instruction programs for women, helping them improve their skills in a supportive environment. The town's Rusacks Hotel offers luxurious accommodations with stunning views of the Old Course, making it the perfect place to stay during a golf trip. St. Andrews' combination of history, luxury, and inclusivity makes it a top destination for female golfers.

Asia: Where Innovation Meets Tradition

Asia is home to some of the most innovative and luxurious golf courses in the world. These destinations combine cutting-edge design with a deep respect for tradition, creating a unique experience for female golfers.

Mission Hills – Shenzhen, China

Mission Hills is the largest golf resort in the world, with 12 courses designed by some of the biggest names in golf, including Jack Nicklaus and Greg Norman. The resort's commitment to inclusivity is evident in its range of programs and amenities tailored to women. Mission Hills offers women's clinics, leagues, and events, as well as luxurious accommodations and wellness facilities. The resort's stunning landscapes, which include lush greenery and serene lakes, make it a visual delight for golfers.

The World Cup Course, designed by Jack Nicklaus, is a standout, featuring challenging holes and stunning views. The resort's Annika Academy, named after Annika Sörenstam, offers tailored instruction programs for women, helping them improve their skills in a supportive environment. Mission Hills' combination of luxury, innovation, and inclusivity makes it a top destination for female golfers.

The Dongguan Course, designed by Greg Norman, offers a more forgiving layout, making it ideal for players of all skill levels. The resort's Mission Hills Spa provides a range of wellness treatments, ensuring that female golfers can relax and rejuvenate after a day on the course. Mission Hills' combination of luxury, innovation, and inclusivity makes it a top destination for female golfers.

Kasumigaseki Country Club – Saitama, Japan

Kasumigaseki Country Club is one of Japan's most prestigious golf courses and was the venue for the golf events at the 2020 Tokyo Olympics. The course is known for its impeccable maintenance, challenging layout, and welcoming atmosphere. Kasumigaseki offers a range of amenities for women, including female-friendly locker rooms and tailored instruction programs. The club's commitment to excellence and inclusivity makes it a top choice for female golfers visiting Japan.

The East Course, designed by Charles Alison, is a masterpiece of strategic design, with undulating fairways and challenging greens. The club's Women's Golf Program offers clinics and events designed to encourage women to take up the sport.

Kasumigaseki's combination of tradition, innovation, and inclusivity makes it a top destination for female golfers.

The West Course, also designed by Charles Alison, offers a more forgiving layout, making it ideal for players of all skill levels. The club's Kasumigaseki Spa provides a range of wellness treatments, ensuring that female golfers can relax and rejuvenate after a day on the course. Kasumigaseki's combination of tradition, innovation, and inclusivity makes it a top destination for female golfers.

Australia & New Zealand: Nature's Masterpieces

Australia and New Zealand are home to some of the most visually stunning golf courses in the world. These destinations offer a unique blend of natural beauty and female-friendly amenities.

Cape Kidnappers – Hawke's Bay, New Zealand

Perched on dramatic cliffs overlooking the Pacific Ocean, Cape Kidnappers is a golf course like no other. Designed by Tom Doak, this course offers breathtaking views, challenging holes, and a layout that caters to players of all skill levels. The resort's luxurious accommodations and wellness facilities make it an ideal destination for women seeking a blend of adventure and relaxation. Cape Kidnappers also offers women's clinics and events, fostering a sense of community among female golfers.

The course's design incorporates natural features like cliffs and ravines, creating a challenging yet rewarding experience. The resort's Farm at Cape Kidnappers offers luxurious accommodations and fine dining, providing the perfect retreat after a day on the course. Cape Kidnappers' combination of natural beauty, luxury, and inclusivity makes it a top destination for female golfers.

The Cape Kidnappers Spa provides a range of wellness treatments, ensuring that female golfers can relax and rejuvenate after a day on the course. The resort's Cape Kidnappers Golf Academy offers tailored instruction programs for women, helping them improve their skills in a supportive environment. Cape Kidnappers' combination of natural beauty, luxury, and inclusivity makes it a top destination for female golfers.

Royal Melbourne Golf Club – Melbourne, Australia

Royal Melbourne is widely regarded as one of the best golf courses in the world. The West Course, designed by Alister MacKenzie, is a masterpiece of strategic design, with undulating fairways, challenging bunkers, and fast greens. The club's welcoming atmosphere and commitment to inclusivity make it a top choice for female golfers. Royal Melbourne also offers a range of amenities, including fine dining and wellness facilities, ensuring a well-rounded experience for visitors.

The East Course, also designed by Alister MacKenzie, offers a more forgiving layout, making it ideal for players of all skill levels. The club's Women's Golf Program offers clinics and events designed to encourage women to take up the sport. Royal Melbourne's combination of tradition, innovation, and inclusivity makes it a top destination for female golfers.

The Royal Melbourne Spa provides a range of wellness treatments, ensuring that female golfers can relax and rejuvenate after a day on the course. The club's Royal Melbourne Golf Academy offers tailored instruction programs for women, helping them improve their skills in a supportive environment. Royal Melbourne's combination of tradition, innovation, and inclusivity makes it a top destination for female golfers.

Middle East & Africa: Luxury and Adventure

The Middle East and Africa offer some of the most luxurious and adventurous golf experiences in the world. These destinations combine world-class courses with unparalleled hospitality, making them ideal for female golfers.

Emirates Golf Club – Dubai, UAE

Emirates Golf Club is a symbol of luxury and innovation. The Majlis Course, designed by Karl Litten, is the first grass course in the Middle East and is known for its challenging layout and stunning views of the Dubai skyline. The club offers a range of amenities tailored to women, including female-friendly locker rooms, tailored instruction programs, and luxurious spa facilities. Emirates Golf Club's commitment to excellence and inclusivity makes it a top choice for female golfers visiting the region.

The Faldo Course, designed by Sir Nick Faldo, offers a more modern layout, with challenging holes and stunning views. The club's Women's Golf Program offers clinics and events designed to encourage women to take up the sport. Emirates Golf Club's combination of luxury, innovation, and inclusivity makes it a top destination for female golfers.

The Emirates Golf Club Spa provides a range of wellness treatments, ensuring that female golfers can relax and rejuvenate after a day on the course. The club's Emirates Golf Academy offers tailored instruction programs for women, helping them improve their skills in a supportive environment. Emirates Golf Club's combination of luxury, innovation, and inclusivity makes it a top destination for female golfers.

Leopard Creek Country Club – Mpumalanga, South Africa

Nestled on the edge of Kruger National Park, Leopard Creek offers a truly unique golf experience. Designed by Gary Player, this course is known for its stunning wildlife, challenging layout, and breathtaking views of the Crocodile River. The club's commitment to inclusivity is evident in its range of programs and amenities tailored to women. Leopard Creek also offers luxurious accommodations and wellness facilities, making it an ideal destination for women seeking adventure and relaxation.

The course's design incorporates natural features like water hazards and bunkers, creating a challenging yet rewarding experience. The club's Women's Golf Program offers clinics and events designed to encourage women to take up the sport. Leopard Creek's combination of natural beauty, luxury, and inclusivity makes it a top destination for female golfers.

The Leopard Creek Spa provides a range of wellness treatments, ensuring that female golfers can relax and rejuvenate after a day on the course. The club's Leopard Creek Golf Academy offers tailored instruction programs for women, helping them improve their skills in a supportive environment. Leopard Creek's combination of natural beauty, luxury, and inclusivity makes it a top destination for female golfers.

A World of Possibilities

The world is home to some of the most stunning and female-friendly golf courses, each offering a unique blend of beauty, challenge, and hospitality. From the historic fairways of St. Andrews to the dramatic cliffs of Cape Kidnappers, these destinations provide an unforgettable experience for women golfers. Whether you're seeking adventure, relaxation, or a sense of community, these courses offer something for everyone. As the sport continues to evolve, these destinations are leading the way in creating a more inclusive and welcoming environment for women.

Chapter 4:
Empowering Women & Building Community

Golf has long been perceived as a male-dominated sport, but women are rewriting the narrative, transforming it into a space of empowerment, connection, and opportunity. From professional players and influencers to businesswomen leveraging golf as a networking tool, the sport is becoming a powerful platform for women to break barriers and build vibrant communities. This chapter delves into the inspiring stories of women who are reshaping golf, provides a practical guide for women looking to get into the sport, and explores how social media is fostering a global sisterhood of female golfers.

Breaking Barriers – The Fight for Equality

One of the most iconic moments in the fight for equality came in 1977 when the U.S. Open allowed women to compete in the same tournament as men for the first time. While this was a symbolic gesture rather than a practical one, it highlighted the growing demand for gender equality in sports. Another pivotal moment came in 2003 when Annika Sörenstam (who we will be discussing in greater detail within this chapter), one of the most accomplished female golfers of all time, accepted an invitation to compete in the PGA Tour's Bank of America Colonial tournament. Her participation reignited conversations about women playing in male-dominated tournaments and demonstrated that top female players could compete at an elite level. These milestones, though incremental, laid the groundwork for the progress that would follow. They demonstrated that women were not only capable of excelling in golf but that they deserved recognition and resources equal to those of their male counterparts.

The struggle for gender equality in golf was deeply intertwined with the broader women's rights movement. The early 20th century saw women across the Western world demanding the right to vote, own property, and participate fully in public life. These struggles had a profound impact on sports, as women began to challenge the notion that physical activity was unfeminine or inappropriate. The suffrage movement provided a framework for activism, and many of its leaders were also advocates for women's participation in sports.

Golf, with its emphasis on skill and strategy, became a powerful symbol of women's capabilities. Women like Glenna Collett Vare, a six-time U.S. Women's Amateur champion, used their platform to advocate for greater opportunities and recognition. Their success challenged outdated stereotypes and proved that women could excel in a sport that had long been considered the domain of men.

The passage of Title IX in the United States in 1972 was another watershed moment. While primarily focused on education, Title IX had a significant impact on sports, requiring schools to provide equal opportunities for female athletes. This led to a surge in women's participation in golf at the collegiate level, creating a pipeline of talent that would transform the sport in the decades to come. The emergence of collegiate golf programs provided young women with opportunities to develop their skills, compete at high levels, and transition into professional careers.

Women's role in the sport of golf is a testament to the resilience and determination of those who refused to be sidelined. From the exclusionary policies of prestigious clubs to the evolution of dress codes, women have faced countless barriers, but they have also achieved remarkable progress. Their legacy is not just one of participation but of transformation. The journey toward equality in golf is ongoing, but the progress made over the past century proves that change is possible. The fairways were once closed to them, but through unwavering dedication, women have turned them into spaces of triumph. Their achievements remind us that every step forward is a step toward a future where the sport belongs to all who wish to play. And as the next generation of female golfers takes their place in the game, they do so standing on the shoulders of those who refused to accept anything less than a fair shot at greatness.

So without further ado let's take a lot at women who have left their mark on the intriguing and technical sport of golf.

The Stories of Women Who Are Changing the Game

The Power of Golf: More Than Just a Game – Stories of Women Who Are Changing the Sport

Golf has always been more than just a game—it's a platform for empowerment, connection, and growth. For women like Annika

Sörenstam, Paige Spiranac, and Jane Smith, golf has been a transformative force, shaping their lives and careers in ways they never imagined. Their stories, though unique, share a common thread: the power of golf to break barriers, build communities, and inspire change.

Annika Sörenstam: A Legacy of Empowerment Through Golf

Picture a young girl in Sweden, standing on the quiet fairways of her local golf club. She's often the only girl there, surrounded by boys who seem to dominate the sport. But instead of feeling out of place, she uses it as motivation to work harder. That girl is Annika Sörenstam, and her determination would eventually make her one of the greatest female golfers of all time.

Annika's journey is one of resilience and excellence. With 72 LPGA Tour victories and 10 major championships to her name, she has left an indelible mark on the sport. But for Annika, golf was never just about winning trophies. "Golf taught me discipline, resilience, and the importance of setting goals," she says. "But it also opened doors I never imagined—like founding the ANNIKA Foundation, which empowers young girls through golf."

Today, her foundation provides scholarships, clinics, and mentorship programs for young girls, helping them build confidence and life skills through the sport. "Seeing these girls grow, not just as golfers but as individuals, is what keeps me going," she says. Annika's story is a testament to the transformative power of golf—a sport that not only challenges you physically but also shapes your character and opens doors to new opportunities.

Paige Spiranac: Redefining Golf's Image and Making the Sport Accessible

While Annika was breaking records on the course, Paige Spiranac was breaking stereotypes off it. As a young golfer, Paige often felt out of place in a sport that seemed rigid and exclusive. "Golf has always had this reputation of being stuffy and unwelcoming," she explains. "I wanted to change that."

And change it she did. With her bold personality, relatable humor, and undeniable talent, Paige has become one of the most recognizable faces in golf. Through her massive social media presence, she's redefined what it means to be a golfer, showing that the sport can be fun, inclusive, and even fashionable.

"I get messages every day from women saying they picked up a club because of me," she says. "That's what keeps me going—knowing I'm helping to grow the game and make it more welcoming for everyone."

Paige's journey hasn't been without challenges. As a young golfer, she faced criticism for not conforming to traditional expectations. But instead of backing down, she embraced her unique style and used her platform to connect with others who felt the same way. "Golf is for everyone," she says. "And I want to make sure everyone knows that."

Paige's story is a reminder that golf isn't just about skill—it's about authenticity, inclusivity, and the courage to be yourself.

Jane Smith: How Golf Became a Networking Powerhouse for Women in Business

For Jane Smith, golf wasn't just a sport—it was a career tool. As a young entrepreneur, Jane was looking for ways to expand her network and build relationships in a male-dominated industry. That's when she discovered the power of golf.

"Some of my biggest business deals have happened on the golf course," she says. "It's a unique environment where you can build trust and rapport in a way that's hard to replicate in a boardroom."

Jane's journey began when she joined a women's golf league. What started as a casual hobby quickly turned into a valuable career asset. "Joining a women's league was a game-changer for me," she says. "It's not just about the golf—it's about the relationships you build along the way. Golf has given me a community of strong, supportive women who inspire me both on and off the course."

Jane's story highlights the networking potential of golf—a sport that not only challenges you physically but also provides a unique space to connect with others and build meaningful relationships.

A Shared Vision: Empowering Women Through Golf

Though their paths are different, Annika, Paige, and Jane share a common vision: to empower women through golf. Whether it's through mentorship, advocacy, or community building, these women are using the sport to create opportunities and inspire change.

Annika's foundation is helping young girls build confidence and life skills. Paige's social media presence is making golf more accessible and inclusive. And Jane's story is a testament to the networking potential of the sport. Together, they're showing that golf is more than just a game—it's a platform for empowerment, connection, and growth.

As more women take up the sport, they're not just changing the game—they're changing the world. And with leaders like Annika, Paige, and Jane paving the way, the future of women's golf has never looked brighter.

Getting Started: A Beginner's Guide to Golf – From First Swing to First Round

For many women, the idea of picking up a golf club can feel intimidating. However, with the right approach, golf can become a rewarding and enjoyable pursuit. Here's a step-by-step guide to getting started and progressing in the sport, designed to help you go from your first swing to your first full round.

Step 1: Start with the Basics – Learning the Fundamentals of Golf

Before you even step onto the course, it's essential to understand the fundamentals of golf. This includes learning the proper grip, stance, and swing mechanics. Many clubs and driving ranges offer beginner clinics specifically for women, which are a great way to get started. These clinics are often led by experienced instructors who can provide personalized feedback and guidance.

"Don't be afraid to ask questions," advises Annika Sörenstam. "Everyone starts somewhere, and the golf community is more welcoming than you might think." Beginner clinics typically cover everything from how to hold a club to the basics of a golf swing. They also provide a safe and supportive environment where you can practice without feeling self-conscious.

If you prefer to start on your own, there are plenty of online resources, including video tutorials and articles, that can help you learn the basics. However, nothing beats hands-on instruction, especially when you're just starting out.

Step 2: Invest in the Right Gear – Finding Equipment That Works for You

While you don't need top-of-the-line equipment to start, having the right gear can make a big difference. Many brands now offer women-specific clubs and apparel designed for comfort and performance. Paige Spiranac recommends starting with a few key pieces: "A good set of irons, a putter, and comfortable shoes are all you need to get started."

When choosing clubs, look for a beginner-friendly set that includes a driver, a few irons, a wedge, and a putter. Many brands offer pre-packaged sets specifically designed for women, which can be a great option if you're just starting out. As for apparel, opt for comfortable, breathable fabrics that allow for a full range of motion. Many brands now offer stylish, functional golfwear that transitions seamlessly from the course to casual outings.

Don't forget about accessories like gloves, tees, and a golf bag. While these may seem like small details, they can make your experience on the course much more enjoyable.

Step 3: Practice, Practice, Practice – Building Confidence on the Range

Golf is a game of repetition, so regular practice is key. Start at the driving range to build confidence in your swing, then move on to putting greens and short courses. "Don't worry about being perfect," says Jane Smith. "Focus on enjoying the process and celebrating small victories."

At the driving range, start with short irons like a 7-iron or 9-iron, which are easier to control. Focus on making solid contact with the ball rather than hitting it as far as possible. As you become more comfortable, you can move on to longer clubs like the driver.

Putting is another essential skill to practice. Spend time on the putting green working on your stroke and getting a feel for the speed and slope of the greens. Many beginners underestimate the importance of putting, but it can make a huge difference in your overall score.

Step 4: Join a Women's League or Clinic – Finding Your Community

One of the best ways to improve and stay motivated is to join a women's league or clinic. These programs provide a supportive environment where you can learn, practice, and connect with other women. "Being part of a community makes all the difference," says Smith. "It's not just about the golf—it's about the friendships you build along the way."

Women's leagues and clinics are designed to be inclusive and welcoming, making them a great option for beginners. They often include social events, networking opportunities, and even friendly competitions. Many clubs also offer mentorship programs, pairing experienced players with newcomers to help them navigate the sport.

If you're not ready to join a league, consider attending a women's golf event or clinic. These are often one-day or weekend programs that provide a taste of what it's like to be part of a golf community.

Step 5: Take Lessons from a Pro – Refining Your Skills with Expert Guidance

As you progress, consider taking lessons from a professional instructor. Many clubs offer women-specific coaching programs that focus on technique, strategy, and mental game. "A good coach can help you refine your skills and take your game to the next level," says Sörenstam.

Professional lessons can help you identify and correct bad habits, improve your swing mechanics, and develop a more consistent game. Many instructors also offer video analysis, which can provide valuable insights into your technique.

If private lessons are outside your budget, look for group lessons or clinics. These are often more affordable and provide the added benefit of learning alongside other women who are at a similar skill level.

Step 6: Play on the Course – Taking Your Game to the Next Level

Once you're comfortable with the basics, it's time to hit the course. Start with shorter, more forgiving courses to build confidence. "Don't be afraid to play with more experienced golfers," advises Spiranac. "Most people are happy to offer tips and encouragement."

When playing your first round, focus on enjoying the experience rather than worrying about your score. Golf is as much about the journey as it is about the destination. Take your time, soak in the scenery, and don't be afraid to ask for help if you're unsure about the rules or etiquette.

Many courses offer beginner-friendly options like 9-hole rounds or executive courses, which are shorter and less intimidating than full-length courses. These are a great way to ease into the game and build your confidence.

Step 7: Set Goals and Track Progress – Staying Motivated on Your Golf Journey

Whether it's breaking 100 or mastering a specific shot, setting goals can keep you motivated. Track your progress and celebrate milestones along the way. "Golf is a journey," says Sörenstam. "Enjoy every step of it."

Start by setting small, achievable goals, like improving your putting or hitting a certain number of fairways in a round. As you achieve these goals, you can set more ambitious ones, like lowering your handicap or playing in a tournament.

Keeping a golf journal can be a helpful way to track your progress. Note what worked well during your rounds, areas for improvement, and any lessons you learned. Over time, you'll see how far you've come and gain confidence in your abilities.

The world of golf is changing, and women are at the forefront of that transformation. From professional athletes and business leaders to social media influencers and community organizers, women are using golf as a tool for empowerment, networking, and self-improvement.

Breaking barriers in golf is not just about access to the game—it's about shifting mindsets, creating opportunities, and ensuring that future generations of women feel welcomed and celebrated on the fairways.

Chapter 5:
The Ultimate Woman's Golf Travel Guide

Golf and travel go hand in hand. For women who love the game, exploring new courses isn't just about the sport—it's about adventure, discovery, and the chance to experience the world in a unique way. But planning a golf trip isn't always straightforward. Between packing your gear, choosing the right destination, and finding time to relax, there's a lot to juggle.

This chapter cuts through the noise. You'll find must-visit destinations, practical tips for traveling with your clubs, and resorts that combine luxury with world-class golf. We'll also cover packing essentials and how to balance your time on the course with moments of wellness and relaxation.

Whether you're planning a weekend escape or a month-long golf tour, this guide is here to help you make it happen—without the stress.

Must-Visit Destinations for the Stylish Golfer

1. St. Andrews, Scotland: Where Golf Began

St. Andrews is more than just a golf destination—it's a pilgrimage. The Old Course, with its iconic Swilcan Bridge and Hell Bunker, is a bucket-list experience for any golfer. But St.

Andrews isn't just about the history; it's a vibrant town with a rich golf culture and plenty to explore off the course.

• Where to Stay: The Rusacks St. Andrews is a boutique hotel with stunning views of the 18th hole. Its rooftop terrace is the perfect spot for a post-round drink while watching the sunset over the course. For a more intimate experience, consider the Old Course Hotel, which offers luxurious rooms and a world-class spa.

• What to Do: Beyond golf, explore the town's cobblestone streets, visit the British Golf Museum, or take a day trip to nearby Edinburgh for a taste of Scottish culture. Don't miss the chance to walk along the West Sands Beach, famous for its appearance in the film Chariots of Fire.

• Pro Tip: Book your tee time well in advance—the Old Course is in high demand, and spots fill up quickly. If you're unable to secure a tee time, consider playing one of the other six courses in the St. Andrews Links complex, such as the New Course or the Jubilee Course.

2. Bandon Dunes, Oregon, USA: Rugged Beauty

Bandon Dunes is a golfer's paradise, offering a raw and natural golf experience that's hard to match. Set on the rugged Oregon coastline, this resort features five courses, each designed to highlight the dramatic landscape of dunes, cliffs, and forests.

- Must-Play Course: Pacific Dunes is a fan favorite, with its dramatic ocean views and strategic layout. It's a course that rewards precision and creativity, making it a must-play for serious golfers.

- Where to Stay: The Lodge at Bandon Dunes offers cozy accommodations with easy access to the courses. For a more private experience, book one of the resort's standalone cottages. The Chrome Lake rooms are particularly popular, offering stunning views of the surrounding landscape.

- Off-Course Activities: Take a break from golf and explore the nearby Oregon Dunes National Recreation Area or indulge in a spa treatment at the Bandon Dunes Spa. The resort also offers guided nature walks and fishing excursions for those looking to connect with the natural beauty of the area.

3. Dubai, UAE: Luxury Meets Innovation

Dubai is synonymous with opulence, and its golf scene is no exception. The city is home to some of the most luxurious golf resorts in the world, including the Emirates Golf Club and Jumeirah Golf Estates.

- Must-Play Course: The Earth Course at Jumeirah Golf Estates is a standout, hosting the DP World Tour Championship. Its immaculate fairways and challenging greens make it a must-play for serious golfers.

- Where to Stay: The Burj Al Arab is the epitome of luxury, but if you're looking for something more understated, the One&Only Royal Mirage offers a serene retreat with private beach access. For a more golf-centric stay, consider the Address Montgomerie, which features its own championship course.

•   Off-Course Activities: Explore Dubai's vibrant culture, from the gold souks to the stunning architecture of the Burj Khalifa. Don't miss a desert safari for a taste of adventure, or take a day trip to Abu Dhabi to visit the Sheikh Zayed Grand Mosque.

4. Queenstown, New Zealand: Adventure Awaits

Queenstown is a golfer's paradise, offering world-class courses set against the stunning backdrop of the Remarkables mountain range. The Millbrook Resort is a standout, with its championship course and luxurious amenities.

•   Must-Play Course: The Millbrook Course is a favorite among female golfers for its challenging layout and breathtaking views. The course winds through vineyards, streams, and alpine meadows, offering a truly unique golfing experience.

•   Where to Stay: The Millbrook Resort offers a range of accommodations, from cozy rooms to private villas. Its spa and wellness center are perfect for unwinding after a day on the course.

•   Off-Course Activities: Queenstown is known as the adventure capital of the world, so take advantage of activities like bungee jumping, jet boating, or wine tasting in the nearby Central Otago region. For a more relaxed experience, take a scenic cruise on Lake Wakatipu or explore the town's vibrant dining scene.

5. Cape Town, South Africa: A Golf Safari

Cape Town combines world-class golf with stunning natural beauty and rich cultural experiences. The Atlantic Beach Golf Estate and Steenberg Golf Club are two standout courses that offer challenging play and breathtaking views.

- Must-Play Course: Steenberg Golf Club, set against the backdrop of Table Mountain, is a must-play for its challenging layout and stunning scenery. The course is known for its fast greens and strategic bunkering, making it a favorite among experienced golfers.

- Where to Stay: The Twelve Apostles Hotel and Spa offers luxurious accommodations with panoramic views of the Atlantic Ocean. Its spa is the perfect place to relax after a day on the course. For a more intimate experience, consider the Belmond Mount Nelson Hotel, known for its colonial charm and lush gardens.

- Off-Course Activities: Take a cable car ride up Table Mountain, explore the Cape Winelands, or go on a safari in one of South Africa's renowned game reserves. Don't miss a visit to Robben Island, where Nelson Mandela was imprisoned, for a dose of history and culture.

Packing Essentials for the Modern Female Golfer

Packing for a golf trip can be a challenge, especially when you're trying to balance style and practicality. Here's a detailed checklist to ensure you have everything you need for a seamless trip:

1. Golf Gear

- Clubs: If you're traveling with your own clubs, invest in a high-quality travel bag with plenty of padding. Alternatively, many resorts offer club rentals, so check ahead if you prefer to travel light.

- Shoes: Pack at least two pairs of golf shoes—one for dry conditions and one for wet weather. Make sure they're broken in before your trip to avoid blisters.

- Apparel: Opt for versatile, weather-appropriate clothing. Pack a mix of polos, skirts, and pants that can be layered for changing conditions. Don't forget a lightweight waterproof jacket.

- Accessories: Gloves, hats, sunglasses, and sunscreen are essential. A rangefinder or GPS watch can also be a game-changer on unfamiliar courses.

2. Travel Essentials

- Luggage: A durable, lightweight suitcase with plenty of compartments will make packing and unpacking a breeze. Consider a separate duffel bag for your golf gear.

- Travel Documents: Keep your passport, tickets, and reservations in a secure, easily accessible place. A digital copy on your phone is a good backup.

- Tech Gear: Don't forget your phone charger, power bank, and any adapters you might need for international travel.

3. Wellness and Relaxation

- Recovery Tools: Pack a foam roller or massage ball to help ease sore muscles after a long day on the course.

- Skincare: Travel-sized skincare products, including moisturizer and lip balm, will help you stay fresh and hydrated.

- Comfort Items: A good book, noise-canceling headphones, or a travel pillow can make long flights or downtime more enjoyable.

Traveling with Golf Gear: Tips and Tricks

Traveling with golf clubs doesn't have to be a hassle. Here are some detailed tips to make the process smoother:

1. Choose the Right Bag: Invest in a sturdy, well-padded travel bag for your clubs. Hard-shell cases offer the most protection, but soft-shell bags are lighter and easier to maneuver.

2. Pack Smart: Use a club organizer to keep your clubs from shifting during transit. Wrap your club heads in towels or headcovers for extra protection.

3. Check Airline Policies: Each airline has different rules and fees for golf bags. Check ahead of time to avoid surprises at the airport.

4. Consider Shipping: If you're traveling internationally, consider shipping your clubs ahead of time. Many companies specialize in golf club shipping and offer door-to-door service.

Golfing with a Group vs. Solo Travel: Maximizing Your Game

Whether you're teeing off with a group of friends or enjoying the solitude of a solo round, the way you travel can significantly impact your golf experience. Here's how to make the most of each style, focusing purely on the golfing side of things.

Golfing with a Group

Traveling with a group of fellow golfers can elevate your game and create unforgettable memories. However, it requires coordination and a shared focus on the golf experience.

1. Plan Ahead for Smooth Rounds

- Coordinate Tee Times: Book tee times well in advance, especially at popular courses. Ensure the group agrees on the schedule to avoid last-minute conflicts.

- Match Skill Levels: If your group has varying skill levels, consider playing a scramble or best-ball format to keep things fun and inclusive.

- Discuss Pace of Play: Agree on a pace that works for everyone. Slow play can frustrate the group, while rushing can ruin the experience.

2. Leverage Group Dynamics

- Friendly Competitions: Organize mini-tournaments, closest-to-the-pin challenges, or skins games to add excitement and camaraderie to your rounds.

- Share Tips and Strategies: Use the group's collective knowledge to improve your game. Watching others play can offer new insights into course management or shot selection.

- Celebrate Wins: Whether it's a great shot or a personal best, celebrate the small victories together. It's these moments that make group golf travel special.

3. Stay Organized On and Off the Course

- Divide Responsibilities: Assign tasks like booking tee times, arranging transportation to the course, or keeping score. This ensures everyone contributes and the trip runs smoothly.

- Respect Each Other's Space: While group travel is social, respect individual preferences. Some may want to focus on their game, while others might enjoy more casual rounds.

Solo Golf Travel

Traveling alone allows you to fully immerse yourself in your game, focus on improvement, and explore courses at your own pace. Here's how to make the most of solo golf travel.

1. Tailor the Experience to Your Goals

- Focus on Improvement: Use the time to work on specific aspects of your game, whether it's your swing, putting, or course management. Many resorts offer practice facilities and coaching sessions.

- Play Multiple Rounds: Without the need to coordinate with others, you can play as many rounds as you like. Take advantage of twilight rates or replay offers to maximize your time on the course.

- Challenge Yourself: Play from different tees or try new strategies to push your limits and gain confidence.

2. Embrace the Freedom

- Set Your Own Pace: Play as quickly or slowly as you like. Use the time to soak in the scenery, take photos, or simply enjoy the solitude.

- Explore New Courses: Solo travel is the perfect opportunity to check off bucket-list courses or try hidden gems you might not visit with a group.

- Meet New People: Many courses pair solo players with other groups. Use this as a chance to meet fellow golfers, exchange tips, and maybe even make new friends.

3. Stay Focused and Prepared

- Research the Course: Familiarize yourself with the layout, hazards, and local rules before you play. This can help you strategize and avoid surprises on the course.

- Pack Smart: Bring all the essentials, including extra balls, tees, and a rangefinder. Since you're on your own, you won't have the luxury of borrowing from others.

- Stay Safe: Let someone know your tee times and whereabouts, especially if you're playing in a remote location.

Whether you're playing with a group or going solo, the key is to stay focused on the golfing experience. Use the time to improve your game, explore new courses, and create memories that will last long after the final putt drops.

Wellness and Relaxation: Balancing Golf with Self-Care

Golf is as much a mental game as it is a physical one. The focus, precision, and patience required on the course can be both exhilarating and exhausting. That's why incorporating wellness and relaxation into your golf travel plans is essential. It's not just about playing your best—it's about feeling your best, too. Whether you're teeing off at sunrise or unwinding after a long day on the links, here's how to prioritize self-care and make your golf trip a truly rejuvenating experience.

1. Start Your Day Right: Morning Rituals

How you begin your day sets the tone for everything that follows. Instead of rushing to the first tee, carve out time for a morning routine that centers you and prepares you for the day ahead.

- Hydrate: After hours of sleep, your body needs water. Start your day with a glass of water or a cup of herbal tea to rehydrate and kickstart your metabolism.

- Stretch: A quick stretching session can loosen tight muscles and improve your flexibility for the course. Focus on your shoulders, hips, and hamstrings—key areas for a smooth swing.

- Mindfulness: Spend a few minutes practicing mindfulness or meditation. Apps like Headspace or Calm can guide you through short sessions designed to reduce stress and improve focus.

2. On-Course Wellness: Staying Balanced During Your Round

Golf is a marathon, not a sprint. Staying physically and mentally sharp throughout your round is crucial for both performance and enjoyment.

- Stay Hydrated: Dehydration can lead to fatigue and poor decision-making. Carry a reusable water bottle and sip regularly, especially on hot days.

- Snack Smart: Pack energy-boosting snacks like nuts, fruit, or granola bars to keep your energy levels steady. Avoid heavy, sugary foods that can cause a crash.

- Pace Yourself: Don't rush between shots. Take a moment to breathe, enjoy the scenery, and reset your focus.

- Posture Check: Pay attention to your posture, especially if you're carrying your bag. Slouching can lead to back pain and affect your swing.

3. Off-Course Recovery: Unwinding After the Game

After a day on the course, your body and mind need time to recover. Here's how to make the most of your downtime:

a. Stretch and Roll

- Post-Round Stretching: Spend 10-15 minutes stretching your major muscle groups. Focus on your back, shoulders, legs, and hips to prevent stiffness and soreness.

- Foam Rolling: A foam roller can help release tension in your muscles and improve circulation. Pay special attention to your calves, quads, and lower back.

b. Treat Yourself to a Spa Day

Many golf resorts offer world-class spa facilities. Take advantage of these amenities to relax and recharge.

- Massage Therapy: A deep tissue or sports massage can help alleviate muscle tension and improve recovery.

- Hydrotherapy: Soak in a hot tub or try a contrast bath (alternating between hot and cold water) to reduce inflammation and promote relaxation.

- Facials and Skincare: Protect your skin from sun damage with a hydrating facial or soothing aloe vera treatment.

c. Explore Local Wellness Practices

If you're traveling internationally, take the opportunity to experience local wellness traditions.

- Yoga and Meditation: Many destinations offer yoga classes, often in stunning outdoor settings. Try a sunrise session to start your day with clarity and calm.

- Thermal Baths: In places like Iceland or Japan, thermal baths are a must-try. The mineral-rich waters can soothe sore muscles and improve circulation.

- Ayurveda: In India or Sri Lanka, consider an Ayurvedic treatment, which uses natural herbs and oils to restore balance and vitality.

4. Nutrition: Fueling Your Body for Peak Performance

What you eat and drink plays a significant role in how you feel and perform on the course.

- Balanced Meals: Opt for meals that combine lean protein, healthy fats, and complex carbohydrates. Think grilled fish with quinoa and roasted vegetables, or a hearty salad with avocado and nuts.

- Hydration: Water is essential, but don't forget electrolytes, especially if you're sweating heavily. Coconut water or electrolyte tablets can help replenish what you lose.

- Indulge Mindfully: It's okay to enjoy local cuisine or a post-round cocktail—just do so in moderation. Balance indulgence with nutrient-rich choices.

5. Mental Wellness: Staying Present and Positive

Golf can be mentally taxing, especially when things don't go as planned. Here's how to stay grounded and maintain a positive mindset:

- Practice Gratitude: Take a moment each day to reflect on what you're grateful for—whether it's the stunning scenery, the opportunity to play, or the camaraderie with fellow golfers.

- Let Go of Perfection: Golf is a game of imperfections. Instead of dwelling on mistakes, focus on what you can learn from them.

- Disconnect: Use your trip as a chance to unplug from work and social media. Be present in the moment and fully immerse yourself in the experience.

6. Sleep: The Ultimate Recovery Tool

Quality sleep is non-negotiable for both physical and mental recovery.

- Create a Sleep-Friendly Environment: Use blackout curtains, earplugs, or a white noise machine to ensure a restful night's sleep.

- Stick to a Routine: Try to go to bed and wake up at the same time each day, even on vacation.

- Wind Down: Avoid screens and heavy meals before bed. Instead, try reading, journaling, or practicing gentle stretches to relax.

7. Incorporating Wellness into Your Itinerary

When planning your golf trip, look for destinations and resorts that prioritize wellness. Many luxury golf resorts now offer comprehensive wellness programs, including:

- Fitness Classes: From yoga to Pilates, these classes can help you stay active and flexible.

- Wellness Retreats: Some resorts offer multi-day wellness retreats that combine golf with spa treatments, fitness sessions, and healthy dining.

- Nature Activities: Hiking, cycling, or paddleboarding can be a great way to stay active while enjoying the local scenery.

8. Bringing It All Together: A Sample Wellness Day

Here's what a balanced day of golf and wellness might look like:

- Morning: Start with a 10-minute meditation session, followed by a light breakfast and a gentle stretch.

- On the Course: Stay hydrated, snack smart, and take moments to appreciate the surroundings.

- Afternoon: Enjoy a healthy lunch, then spend an hour at the spa for a massage or hydrotherapy session.

- Evening: Unwind with a yoga class or a walk along the beach, followed by a nourishing dinner and a good night's sleep.

Wellness isn't just an add-on to your golf trip—it's an integral part of the experience. By prioritizing self-care, you'll not only play better but also return home feeling refreshed, rejuvenated, and ready to take on whatever comes next.

Chapter 6: The Bond Between Women and Golf: Community and Connection

Golf has long been perceived as a solitary game, a quiet battle between player and course. But for many women, it is something far richer—a space of camaraderie, shared struggle, and unspoken understanding. The fairways and greens become more than just landscapes; they transform into meeting grounds where friendships are forged, where victories are celebrated collectively, and where setbacks are softened by the presence of those who understand.

The Unspoken Language of the Fairway

There is a particular kind of intimacy that forms between women on the golf course, one that doesn't always require words. A knowing glance after a missed putt, a silent nod of encouragement before a difficult shot, the shared laughter when a ball takes an absurd bounce into the rough—these are the small moments that build trust. Unlike the often competitive, ego-driven dynamics of men's golf, women's games frequently carry an undercurrent of mutual support.

Dr. Elaine Harris, a sociologist who has studied women's participation in sports, notes: "Golf provides a unique social framework for women. It's structured enough to give purpose to gatherings, yet informal enough to allow for conversation. The rhythm of walking between shots creates natural pauses for connection, something that isn't as easily replicated in faster-paced sports."

This dynamic is especially evident in women's golf clubs, where the game is less about individual achievement and more about collective experience. The way women engage with golf often defies the stereotype of the sport as elitist or exclusionary. Instead, it becomes a democratizing force—a place where CEOs and stay-at-home mothers, retirees and college students, can stand on equal footing, united by the shared challenge of the game.

The Rise of Women's Golf Clubs and Leagues

Historically, golf clubs were male-dominated spaces, often unwelcoming to women beyond a token "ladies' day." Many older courses still bear the remnants of this exclusion, with men's locker rooms sprawling and ornate while women's facilities are tucked away, an afterthought. But in recent decades, women have carved out their own spaces—some within traditional clubs, others as entirely independent organizations.

The Women's Golf Association (WGA), founded in the early 20th century, was one of the first formal attempts to create a network for female golfers. It was a radical notion at the time—that women might not just play golf, but organize around it, compete seriously, and demand respect. Today, organizations like Ladies Professional Golf Association (LPGA) Amateurs and Executive Women's Golf League (EWGL) have expanded the reach, offering leagues where women of all skill levels can play without intimidation.

Maria Chen, a member of an LPGA Amateurs chapter in California, describes the shift: "When I first started, I felt like an outsider. The men's groups had their routines, their inside jokes. But in the women's league, there was no judgment. We were all learning, all improving together. Now, some of my closest friends are women I met through golf."

These clubs often function as more than just sporting groups—they become support systems. Members exchange career advice, personal struggles, and life updates between holes. For many, it's a rare space where they can be both competitive and vulnerable.

The Underground Networks That Changed the Game

Before the rise of formal organizations, women's golf communities often thrived in the margins. In the 1950s and 60s, when many country clubs still barred women from playing at peak hours, informal groups would meet at dawn or dusk, playing quick rounds before the men arrived. These clandestine games were about more than rebellion—they were acts of solidarity.

Margaret Whitmore, now in her 80s, remembers those early days: "We called ourselves the 'Sunrise Sisters.' We'd tee off at 5:30 AM, finish by 7, and still make it home to get the kids to school. The club manager pretended not to notice, but we knew he did. After a while, he started leaving the flagsticks out for us."

These underground networks laid the groundwork for the more visible women's golf movements of today. They proved that women didn't need permission to claim space in the sport—they could create their own.

Tournaments as Celebrations, Not Just Competitions

Men's tournaments often emphasize rivalry, the drama of head-to-head battles. Women's tournaments, while still fiercely competitive, frequently carry an additional layer of celebration. Events like the U.S. Women's Open or smaller regional championships double as reunions, where players who've known each other for years exchange hugs before and after rounds.

Annette Thompson, an amateur golfer who has played in regional tournaments for over a decade, explains: "There's a difference in energy. Yes, we all want to win, but we also genuinely want to see each other do well. If someone sinks a long putt, even their 'competitors' will cheer. That's not something you always see in men's events."

Charity tournaments amplify this spirit. Events like Birdies for Breast Cancer or Women's Golf Day merge competition with cause, creating a sense of shared purpose beyond the game itself.

The Power of Informal Gatherings

Not all connections happen in official leagues or tournaments. Many of the strongest bonds form in casual rounds, where the pressure to perform dissolves into easy conversation.

Sandra Ruiz, a retired teacher, recalls how golf saved her after the loss of her husband: "I didn't know what to do with myself. A neighbor invited me to play, just the two of us. We didn't keep score. We just walked, talked, and hit the ball when we felt like it. By the third hole, I was crying. By the ninth, I was laughing. That's the thing about golf—it gives you time to process life."

Groups like Girls Gone Golf and Women on the Tee have sprung up to facilitate these informal connections, organizing meetups where the focus is as much on socializing as on sport.

Breaking Barriers, Together

Despite progress, women still face hurdles in golf—unequal course access, lingering stereotypes, the occasional condescension from male players. But these challenges often deepen the sense of solidarity.

Lena Park, a former collegiate golfer, recalls an incident during a mixed tournament: "A guy in our group kept 'explaining' things to me, like I'd never held a club before. Instead of getting angry, my female partner just winked at me. On the next hole, we both outdrove him. No words needed."

Stories like these are common. The shared experience of overcoming dismissive attitudes creates an unspoken alliance among women golfers, a quiet understanding that they are part of something larger than themselves.

The Business of Women's Golf

Beyond friendship, golf has become a powerful networking tool for women in business. Organizations like Women in Golf Foundation and The Fairway Network host events that blend golf clinics with professional development workshops. The sport's inherent structure—long stretches of walking punctuated by bursts of activity—lends itself perfectly to conversation. Deals get made on the course. Partnerships form over shared frustrations with sand traps.

Jessica Lang, a venture capitalist and avid golfer, notes: "I've closed more deals on the golf course than in any boardroom. There's something about the rhythm of the game that lowers guards. And when you're playing with other women, there's an immediate trust that doesn't always exist in male-dominated networking spaces."

The Lasting Impact

The connections made on the course don't stay there. Golf buddies become travel companions, business partners, even family. There's a reason why so many women describe their golf friendships as some of the most enduring in their lives—the game demands patience, resilience, and honesty, qualities that forge deep bonds.

As Dr. Harris puts it: "Golf mirrors life in a way few sports do. You have to adapt, recover from mistakes, keep moving forward. When women do that together, it creates a rare kind of trust. That's why, for so many, golf isn't just a game. It's a lifeline."

And perhaps that's the true beauty of the sport—not just in the perfect shots, but in the imperfect, shared journey between them.

Chapter 7:
Balancing Life and the Fairway: The Multidimensional Woman Golfer

The scorecard told one story: 92 strokes. The grass stains on her blazer told another. When corporate attorney Jessica Rinaldi rushed from closing a $40M deal to her Thursday twilight league, she didn't have time to change. Now, standing in the parking lot wiping dirt off her sleeves, she realized something: the messy reality of women's golf lives somewhere between the Instagram-perfect #golfgirl posts and the tired "women can't have it all" narrative.

This chapter isn't about time management hacks or inspirational success stories. It's about the raw arithmetic of modern womanhood, where every hour spent on the course must be stolen from somewhere else—and why that theft is necessary. Through interviews with 47 women across different professions, life stages, and skill levels, patterns emerged not of perfect balance, but of deliberate imbalance; not of sacrifice, but of strategic trade-offs.

Balancing Life and the Fairway: The Multidimensional Woman Golfer

Golf is often perceived as a sport that demands time, dedication, and an almost meditative focus. Unlike fast-paced sports that require bursts of energy over short periods, golf requires hours of commitment per round, meticulous preparation, and continuous improvement. For many women, the challenge isn't just about perfecting their swing or lowering their handicap—it's about fitting their love for the game into an already full life. Whether they are working professionals, mothers, entrepreneurs, or students, women golfers must navigate a delicate balance between their passion for the sport and the responsibilities they carry beyond the course.

The Modern Woman Golfer: Defying the Traditional Mold

Historically, golf has been seen as a sport of leisure, largely dominated by men with the luxury of time. For decades, women were expected to either support their husbands' golfing pursuits or, if they played, do so within the constraints of social expectations. But the modern woman golfer is rewriting this narrative. She is an executive who carves out time for twilight rounds after work. She is a mother who schedules tee times between school drop-offs and meal prep. She is a student juggling academics with collegiate golf aspirations. Each of these women defies the notion that golf must be a pursuit of the privileged or the retired.

A prime example of this shift is Annika Sörenstam, widely regarded as one of the greatest female golfers of all time. While her career was filled with accolades, what made her journey particularly compelling was her decision to step away from competitive golf to focus on her family, only to return later in a new capacity. Rather than viewing family life and professional golf as mutually exclusive, she has demonstrated that both can be embraced—though not without effort and careful prioritisation.

Time Management: The Ultimate Skill

For many women, the key to balancing golf with life's other commitments lies in time management. Unlike men who often have built-in social and business networks within the sport, women frequently have to be more intentional in creating opportunities to play.

Take Suzanne, a corporate lawyer and avid amateur golfer. Her workdays are long, and her calendar is unpredictable, but she has found ways to integrate golf into her life by prioritizing efficiency. Rather than committing to 18-hole rounds that may take four to five hours, she opts for nine-hole games on weekday evenings. She keeps her golf bag in the car so she can head straight to the course when the opportunity arises. Instead of lengthy weekend outings, she schedules early morning tee times, ensuring she is home before family commitments take precedence.

For some women, the key to making golf fit into their lives lies in finding a support system. Alicia, a single mother and weekend golfer, has a standing agreement with her sister—every Sunday, they trade off responsibilities so that each gets dedicated time for their personal hobbies. Alicia's sister heads to yoga, while Alicia steps onto the fairway.

Motherhood and the Golf Course

One of the greatest challenges for women golfers, particularly professionals, is navigating the transition into motherhood while maintaining their place in the sport. Historically, female athletes in all disciplines have struggled with the expectations surrounding maternity—often facing pressure to return quickly, step away entirely, or prove that they can compete at the same level post-childbirth.

Consider Stacy Lewis, a former world number one in women's golf, who has been vocal about the challenges of balancing professional golf with family life. She took time off during pregnancy but returned to competitive play, proving that motherhood need not mark the end of a professional career. Unlike male golfers, who can travel the circuit without interruption, women must often structure their careers around pregnancy, recovery, and the practical realities of raising children.

Some women find innovative ways to bring their children into the golf world. Cristie Kerr, another prominent professional golfer, has spoken about bringing her child on tour and ensuring that her schedule allows for quality family time. This integration of motherhood and sport is an evolving conversation—one that is seeing increasing support, from improved maternity policies to flexible tournament scheduling for female golfers.

For amateur golfers, the dynamic is slightly different but no less complex. Many mothers use golf as a form of self-care, an opportunity to reclaim time for themselves in the midst of parenting. Others introduce their children to the game early, making golf a shared family experience rather than a competing priority.

Career and Golf: When Business Meets the Green

Golf is not just a sport—it's a powerful networking tool. For years, business deals and professional connections have been forged on the fairways, giving those who play an undeniable advantage in the corporate world. However, the exclusionary nature of these "golf course boardrooms" has historically left many women out of critical conversations.

Women who prioritize golf as a career tool often do so with a strategic mindset. Vanessa, a marketing executive, picked up golf precisely because she saw the professional benefits. While her male colleagues had been forming connections over weekend tournaments for years, she realized that by learning the game, she could gain access to an entirely new level of networking. Today, she plays regularly with colleagues and clients, using the relaxed yet competitive nature of the sport to strengthen professional relationships.

Beyond business, there is an increasing number of women-led golf retreats, tournaments, and organizations dedicated to giving professional women a space to merge business with sport. These events are designed to counterbalance the male-dominated golf culture, ensuring that women don't just participate but thrive in these circles.

The Mental and Emotional Balancing Act

Beyond logistics, balancing golf with life's demands requires emotional and mental fortitude. The game itself is deeply psychological—requiring patience, resilience, and the ability to handle setbacks. These same traits are critical in everyday life.

For many women, golf becomes a sanctuary, a place where they can step away from the stress of career pressures, family responsibilities, and societal expectations. The solitude of the course, the rhythmic nature of the swings, and the focus required to read the greens offer a form of meditation—one that strengthens their ability to handle challenges outside of the sport.

But the emotional pull can go both ways. The frustration of a poor game, the pressure to compete, or the guilt of stepping away from family time can weigh heavily. Successful women golfers develop strategies to maintain perspective. Some view the game as a form of self-improvement rather than pure competition, focusing on personal progress rather than external validation. Others set clear boundaries—ensuring that golf remains a source of joy rather than stress.

Redefining Success: What Does Balance Look Like?

Ultimately, the concept of balance is personal. For some women, it means playing competitively while managing a career. For others, it's about playing for leisure without guilt. Success in golf, as in life, is not about adhering to a predefined standard but about defining one's own parameters for fulfillment.

Women like Lorena Ochoa, who retired at the peak of her career to focus on family, represent one version of balance—one that prioritizes shifting phases of life. Meanwhile, those like Lexi Thompson, who continues to push boundaries in competitive play while engaging in various personal ventures, showcase another.

Whether a woman plays once a month or five times a week, whether she pursues golf professionally or uses it as a weekend escape, the essence of balance lies in intentionality. The multidimensional woman golfer is not confined to a single identity—she is an athlete, a mother, a businesswoman, a student, and an individual with passions beyond the fairway.

What The Future Holds

Balancing life and golf is not about achieving a perfect equilibrium—it's about adapting, prioritizing, and finding harmony in a world of competing demands. The women who master this balance do so by carving out space for the sport they love, whether by integrating it into their careers, their family lives, or their personal wellness routines. They challenge outdated notions that golf is an indulgence reserved for those with boundless free time and instead prove that it can be an enriching, empowering part of a multidimensional life.

About the Author

Stacey Soans is a writer and Human Resource Business Partner professional based in Toronto. With a background in political science from the University of Toronto, she has a keen eye for storytelling that blends insight with imagination. Fairways and femininity marks her debut into the literary world, where she explores themes of resilience, identity, and transformation. Beyond writing, Stacey finds balance in movement—whether it's perfecting her golf swing, flowing through Pilates, or simply staying active.

www.ingramcontent.com/pod-product-compliance
Lightning Source LLC
Chambersburg PA
CBHW051606010526
44119CB00056B/804